THE RULERS

Benjamin Marshall

At the beginning of the creation of the world, there were three rulers. God, the ruler of light in heaven. Satan, the ruler of darkness - the place where God is not. Man was created by God as the ruler of the earth.

The ruler of earth was supposed to rule the earth like the ruler of Heaven, God. The ruler of darkness tempted the man to rule it like he would. The man, ruler of earth, gave his will to rule like the ruler of darkness so the world became a dark place without much light.

The ruler of heaven knew what would happen to the man who was to rule the earth. He refused to allow this darkness to rule man forever. In the meantime, the man, whose rulership was taken, would need to seek Him if he wanted to fix his situation and break free from this darkness.

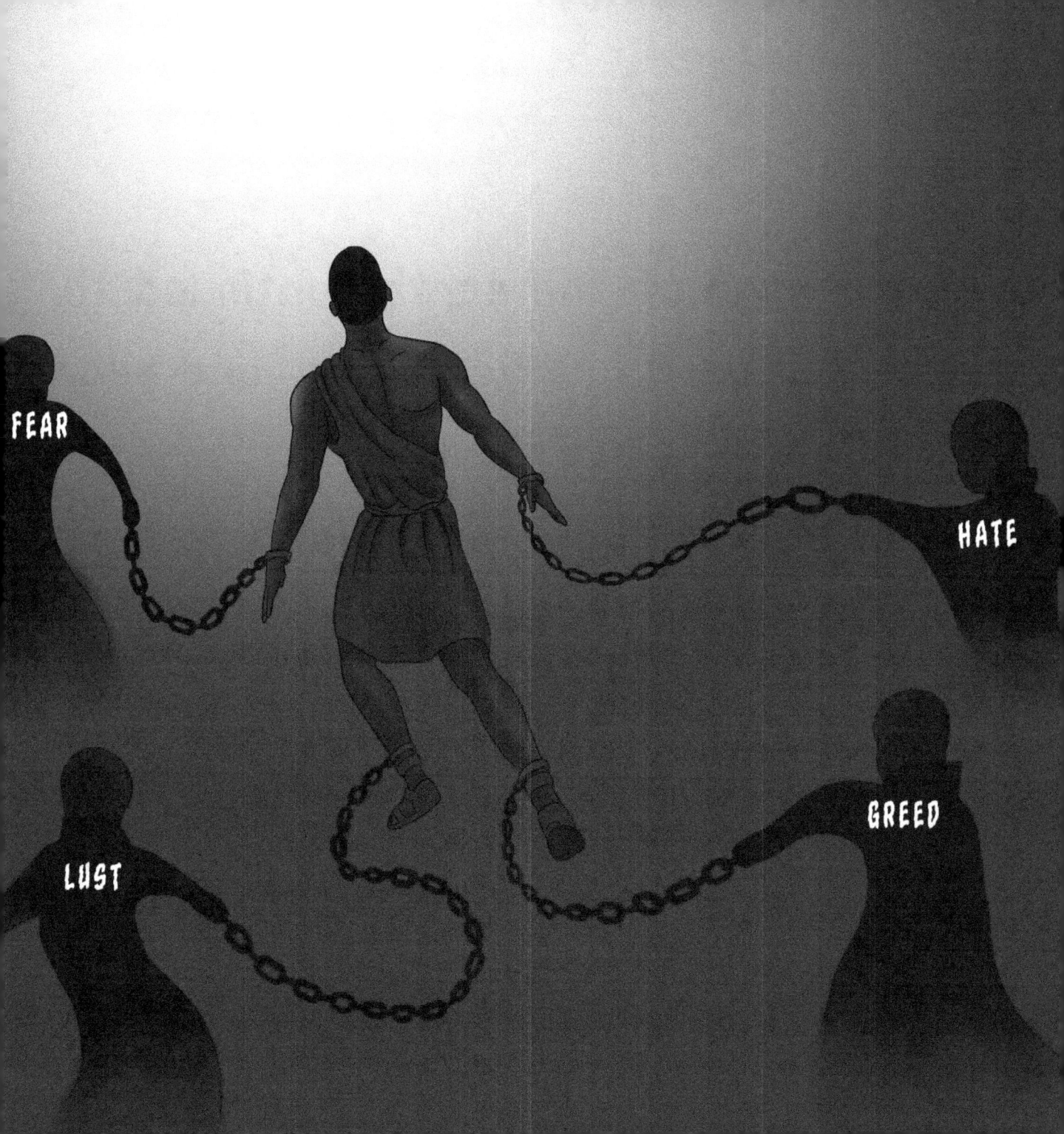

As this man of the earth continued to search for good, justice, love, and peace in this world, some would eventually find it. The ruler of light would intervene and allow himself to be found by those seeking truth.

After a chosen few through the ages had found him, he put his master plan to work. He would make it very easy for anyone to find him. He would come to the earth himself.

Now the earth would require him to be formed into a being like those he made to rule it. He would change into their form but without losing who He was.

Once he arrived on the earth, he would resist the darkness and even reverse many things it was responsible for; like blindness, lameness, sadness, sickness, but most importantly sinfulness – the acts of doing wrong.

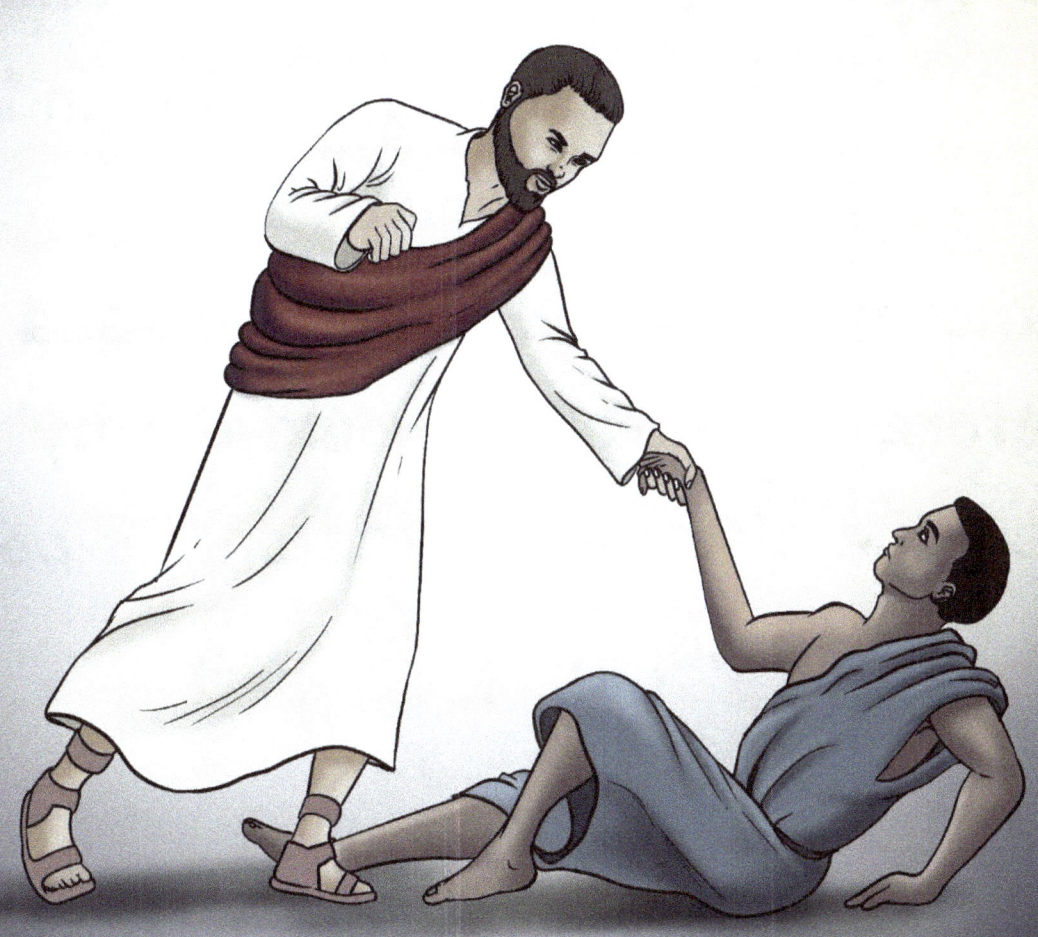

He could only stay for awhile and there was so much still to be done and what about those who would come later. He thought it out. He had decided that before his exit, he would die by taking everyone else bad deeds on his body and rid them this way.

So, He gathered all the wrongs that was ever done and will ever be and He took them, poured them on himself, suffering and allowing this evil to kill Him instead of them. It was a sad day as His family, friends, and followers tried to understand what happened. Then, they buried Him.

All had seemed lost but this great ruler of light knew what He would do. He had a power the ruler of darkness misunderstood. He had the power over sin and death, man's final enemy. He came alive again.

He did this for the man who was made the first ruler of the earth. Man could now no longer live in fear of his life ending in a bad way. He could fix his life on earth and when he was done, he would be able to rule again with this ruler of light without the threat of darkness ever again.

Before the ruler of light left, He showed himself to His friends and told them, "You must now rule. Now go and tell everyone you can what I did for them. Everyone who wants the light, another chance, and eternal life, must only believe in me."

Who was He? What is His name? His name is Jesus, the Christ.

For God so loved the world, that he gave his only son, that whoever believes in him shall not perish but have everlasting life.

John 3:16

God loves you so much. Please accept his free gift of love. If you believe in your heart and confess with your mouth Jesus Christ as Lord, you will be saved. Pray this prayer:

Father God in Heaven, I come to you now. I am a sinner and in need of your help. Please forgive me of all my bad deeds. I believe you sent your son Jesus Christ to earth. I believe he died for my sins. I believe he rose again. I accept Him as my Savior and Lord. Thank you for giving me eternal life today. Now fill me with your spirit so I can live the life you want. In Jesus name I pray. Amen.

ABOUT THE AUTHOR

International teacher, speaker, and humanitarian, Benjamin Marshall is founder of Seeds of Truth Academy. His ministry and educational center extend worldwide. He has been blessed with four natural children and many God children.

For other books and information contact him: sotacademy@gmail.com

www.ingramcontent.com/pod-product-compliance
Lightning Source LLC
Chambersburg PA
CBHW080120020526
44112CB00037B/2813